The Daisy Chain

By Richard Jones
And Daisy Walton

The Daisy Chain

Spiderwize
Remus House
Coltsfoot Drive
Woodston
Peterborough
PE2 9BF

www.spiderwize.com

Whilst The Daisy Chain is inspired by true events some details and incidents have been elaborated for dramatic purposes. Apart from Daisy herself all of the other names of characters are fictional. Many thanks to Daisy's parents Ian and Tracey Walton for their unstinting support and the use of Ian's poem 'I Taught Her'; to the team at Bonacia for patiently guiding the project through to publication and to Richard's wife Corinne for incisive critical comment and such a clever title described by Daisy as 'wicked'!

ISBN: 978-1-908128-88-1

Garnet Starling embraces the Earth

Cast

Daisy and five Chorus actors

Production notes

The Daisy Chain is a concise text with plenty of opportunities for young actors and directors to develop their own style and interpretation.
For this reason staging and direction notes are minimal and are usually merely conveying necessary character information or logistical points.

Many of the monologues are printed in a continuous style and the merits of this were discussed at the pre-publication stage.
More traditional punctuation and paragraphing were considered but I would prefer young actors to find their own rhythms and pacing rather than be influenced by my own ideas. It might be worth looking at texts which use the oblique (/) mark to break up speeches in a poetic style. My edition of Berkoff's 'West' uses this method and I would encourage students and young actors to experiment with inserting their own oblique marks to discover how this can alter the delivery.

Indeed the Berkovian style would certainly be an excellent starting point for The Daisy Chain. I recall listening to Steven Berkoff in conference describing how, in his production of Coriolanus, he used a group of actors to physicalise the powerful moment when a great door was opened rather than have the physical apparatus of a door on the set. I can only imagine how impressive this moment would have been and would urge you to adopt a similar approach to this text.
For example, the references to Daisy's earth name *Garnet Starling Embraces the Earth* and the Native American proverb *'The journey in between what you once were and who you are now becoming is where the dance of life takes place'* would burst into life with imaginative physical representation. These could be your 'Coriolanus door' moments and an exercise I favour for such work is called 'The Flock of Birds.'
This is an ensemble movement exercise developed by the French physical theatre specialist Jacques le Coq. I would certainly recommend research of his work.

Finally, The Daisy Chain should be stimulating, challenging and charming. Please make it your own. There is no performance fee; I want to empower work not hinder it. Just buy a few copies of the script rather than photocopy (you know who you are, you naughty Drama teachers!) However, above all else, please do let me know about your amazing productions and workshop ideas. I can't wait to see what can be made of it. The early part of this journey discussing Daisy's experiences with her was remarkable and inspirational. Please contact me on Twitter @Richard_Jones63 to let me know how the next leg of this remarkable journey develops.

Richard Jones

How it all began

Section 1

All of the chorus enter and form a line facing the audience. They each wear a plain white mask. They remove their masks simultaneously. These will need to be placed in a convenient part of the stage for the final scene; a problem probably best solved by each individual cast.

Chorus 2

I taught her how to smile:
She laughed at me.
I taught her how to talk:
She shouted at me.
I taught her how to walk:
She ran away.

Chorus 1 *(As a Head Teacher on the phone)*

Good afternoon. Is that Daisy's mum?

Chorus 5 *(As Daisy's mum)*

Speaking.

Chorus 1

Oh hello, it's Mr Black here. Daisy's head teacher.

Chorus 5

Oh, no! What's she done now?

Chorus 1

Well I'd rather not talk about it on the phone. Would you be able to come in and see me?

Chorus 2 *(Like a pupil offering a cigarette)*

Hey Daisy. Take a drag on that.

Chorus 4 *(As if offering a bottle to drink out of)*

Take a swig of that. I nicked it from Tesco.

Chorus 1
Good afternoon. Is that Daisy's mum?

Chorus 2
Take a drag on that.

Chorus 4
All the alarms went off. I had to run like shit. I chucked it over the fence and climbed over. The fat bastard security guard couldn't catch me.

Chorus 5
What's she done now?

Chorus 4
Take a swig.

Chorus 2
Take a drag.

Chorus 1
Would you be able to come in and see me?

Chorus 3
You're going to get a tattoo?

Chorus 5
What's she done now?

Chorus 4
Take a swig.

Chorus 3
A fucking tattoo!

Chorus 1
Good afternoon. Is that Daisy's mum?

(The whole chorus now go on to all speak the following lines all at the same time.)

Chorus 1
Good afternoon. Is that Daisy's mum?

Chorus 2
Take a drag on that.

Chorus 3
A fucking tattoo!

Chorus 4
I nicked it from Tesco.

Chorus 5
What's she done now?

(It becomes difficult to hear what everyone is saying. It builds to a crescendo until finally Daisy walks on in front of them all wearing the clothes she wore on camp in America and carrying her over loaded ruck sack.)

Daisy *(Shouting)*
Stop!

(But the chorus don't stop. She shouts again)

Stop right now!

(This time the chorus do stop and freeze into a still image. Daisy addresses the audience.)

Daisy

Have you ever got to the stage where your life's in a mess? I mean a real mess. I did. And I didn't really know it either. It's like if I emptied this ruck sack all over the floor now it'd make a mess. A big mess. I've got a lot of stuff in there. But it still wouldn't be as big a mess as I was in.

(She takes off her ruck sack and makes like she is thinking whether or not to do this demonstration. The audience must wonder whether she will or not. After some consideration she does. She empties the whole contents of her bag all over the floor. She surveys the scene.)

No. I was in a bigger mess than this. I'd been a bad girl. A really bad girl. And I was only fourteen by this stage. So how bad can a girl be? Well of course there was drinking. Most of it was stolen. We had to start wearing disguises when we went in Tesco.

(As she starts to describe her misdemeanours she packs relevant items back into the bag e.g a tin drinks container represents the stolen alcohol)

And there was smoking.

(The chorus now come to life as her school friends)

Chorus 2

Anyone for a drag on this?

Chorus 1

What is it?

Chorus 2

It's good stuff.

Chorus 3

Where d'you get it from?

Chorus 2
We ent grassing no one.

Daisy *(Aside to the audience)*
You might have guessed we're not just talking fags here.

Chorus 2
Try that Daisy.

Chorus 3
Come on Daisy!

Daisy
  (To the audience. The other actors freeze)

Now you might be feeling a bit sorry for me here. These guys were really pushing this stuff on me. They were older kids. They should have known better. I was young. Easily led.

Easily led my arse. It wasn't like that at all. I was the fuckin' ring leader.

  (She goes back into the scene)

Anyone for a drag on this?

Chorus 1
What is it?

Daisy
It's good stuff.

Chorus 3
Where d'you get it from?

Daisy
I ent grassing no one.

(To the audience)

And then there was the sex.

(Chorus 4 picks up the sleeping mat from the ruck sack and rolls it out. He lies on it on his back with his head towards the audience. Daisy straddles him, puts her hands either side of his head and gives him a passionate kiss. She looks up to the audience)

I know! And I was only fourteen!

(She gets off him. He stands up with his back to the audience and mimes doing up his flies. He walks off)

Daisy *(Calling after him)*
Same time next week?

Have I told you about the tattoo incident yet?

(During this the actor playing Daisy performs both Daisy and Bof, the tattooist)

You'll love this one but there is a moral to the tale. I know what you're thinking. Daisy? Moral? Anyway. There was this guy who lived in the village and he did dodgy tattoos in his garage. When I say dodgy I mean no questions asked. That sort of thing. Now in theory you have to be eighteen to have a tattoo. Or sixteen with your parents' permission. But who gets parents' permission for anything? So I go and see this guy. Bof, his name was. Nothing else. Just Bof. Don't ask me why. He was a bit of a hippy. Long hair. Goatee beard. 'Hi there dude,' he says. 'So what sort of thing can I do you for?' 'Well, I was thinking about a bird. Maybe a robin. I like robins.' 'Yeah, cool man. I can do robins.' And off he goes to work.

(The actor does the buzzing sound of the needle and mimes Bof approaching to make his first mark)

Daisy

'Fuck!' I shouted out. 'Sorry man. You'll get used to the pain,' Bof tried to reassure me. If anyone ever says to you tattoos are painless, don't believe them. So he carries on. And I do get used to it. A bit. Until suddenly... Bzzzzzzzz! Aitchoo! He sneezes and slips. 'Oh man!' And then he goes quiet. 'Is everything OK?' 'I just slipped man' 'And?' 'I just put an extra little bit in by mistake' 'Let me see' 'It'll be fine.' 'Fuck off! Let me see!' So he holds up a mirror.

(She mimes him holding up a mirror with her trying to get a good view of the side of her rib cage)

'Shit! It looks like it's got a big cock!' 'I was trying to do a foot man.' 'Well it doesn't look like a foot' 'I think I can rectify it' 'Rectify it my arse!' And at that point I walked out. Well I sort of stormed out. I didn't even pay him. He didn't dare ask. And so I come to the moral of the tale boys and girls. If you're considering a tattoo, even an illegal one, make sure you get it done by a professional. Not some hippy in a garage. I speak from experience as I am now the only girl in town who is the proud owner of a tattoo of a robin with a six inch penis. It even has an erection when I lift my arm up.

(She mimes lifting her arm up. The lifting of the arm turns into a dance move as the scene cuts to loud party music. The chorus and Daisy all dance in a teenage way. They have all obviously had too much to drink etc. Daisy eventually comes to the audience while it's all still going on. She has to shout very loudly to make herself heard)

Daisy

I'm havin' a party. I said I'm havin' a party. Got some mates round. The neighbours don't like it.

(Abrupt cut of the music. The chorus all stand straight like respectable residents from the neighbourhood. As one they speak)

Chorus

Turn that noise down!

Daisy
Fuck off!

(The music restarts as abruptly as it stopped and all the chorus become the teen party goers again)

Daisy *(Having to shout again to make the audience hear her)*
Mum and Dad were away. But it was still only a party. Lots of teenagers have their mates round when their parents are away. What could possibly go wrong?

(The music cuts again but this time the chorus freeze exactly where they are in their dance moves)

Daisy
Allow me to explain. We all know kids who have spilled the odd drink on Mummy and Daddy's nice dining room table while they were out. Maybe something on the carpet. Or the ceiling. Or puke on the bathroom floor. Or a cracked sink basin. I'm sure it's all happened and might have cost a few quid to put right. But how about a repair bill for twenty-five grand? Yes! You heard me! You see, we've got this extension with a flat roof. You can get to it by climbing out my bedroom window. I mean! Why dance in the house when you can dance on the roof? At least it didn't matter if we spilt anything. Although it turned out that fifty kids on the roof was a bit too much for it. I'm no engineer but it sort of makes sense. It's a miracle nobody was killed.

(At this point she walks through the chorus and talks about each one. The names can be changed to suit the ratio of boys to girls in the chorus)

Jack was the first to go through. It started off with a small crack beneath his feet. But it opened up real quick. Sarah went through after him. Broken wrist. And the crack just spread like a mini earth quake. I was in my bedroom at the time with, well, you don't need to know but I was in my bedroom. I looked up to see Charlie disappear followed by Nikki. She pulled all her finger nails off trying to hold on. Tom came off worst. Broken collar bone. Ouch! The earth certainly moved for me that night. So much so that my big sister decided it was time for things to change.

Daisy
What are big sisters for?

(Daisy sits in a different part of the stage hugging her knees to her chest. She is supposedly alone in her bedroom. Mum, Dad and sister have the following conversation 'downstairs')

Chorus 3 *(Sister)*
So what do you think?

Chorus 5 *(Mum)*
How long would it be for?

Chorus 3
As long as it takes.

Chorus 1 *(Dad)*
It's a hell of a lot of money.

Chorus 3
Worth it if it works.

Chorus 5
Would she be able to come on holiday with us?

Chorus 3
Probably not.

Chorus 1
If we're spending all this money why don't we just find another school for her?

Chorus 3
You've tried that before.

Chorus 5
My baby!

Chorus 3
My little sisiter.

Chorus 1
I taught her how to smile.

Chorus 5
Shouldn't Daisy have a say in this?

Chorus 3
I don't think she's capable of it. I don't think she knows what's best for her.

Chorus 1
We'll have to present it as a positive experience. Something to look forward to.

Chorus 5
I'm not sure how she'll take it.

Chorus 3
Let me talk to her first.

Daisy (*Shouting downstairs*)
I'm not deaf! Or stupid! I can hear you talking about me.

(*To the audience*)

They were packin' me off to the US of fucking A.

(*Daisy moves to the side*)

Chorus 3 *(Miming using a lap top)*
RedCliff Ascent

(The other chorus stand behind Chorus 3 in a line 'being' the words that Chorus 3 reads on the screen. They should do American accents)

Chorus 2
'RedCliff Ascent is a leader in providing clinically sophisticated wilderness therapy for troubled teens ages 13-17. For many years we have served thousands of troubled teens and their families, helping them realise their potential and rebuild their lives.'

Chorus 5
'We must meet each and every student's needs and potential.'

Chorus 4
'Experiential activities are the foundation of therapeutic success. Therapy is not about sitting on a couch and talking about the problems in life. It is about touching, feeling, smelling and seeing what life has to offer. Through experiential activities, students manifest their true emotions and behaviours as an individual and peers.'

Chorus 1
'We must always remember that we have been entrusted with the care of a child by loving parents who have suffered and sacrificed to place their child in our care.'

Daisy
It was time to get me some Wilderness Therapy.

For the first leg of the journey Me, Mum and Dad went down to Stanstead. We stayed in a hotel and had a slap up meal the night before they came for me. When I say 'they' it was like two former US cops. Seriously! This was heavy stuff!

Chorus 1 *(Daisy's dad)*
I couldn't bear to see her go. My little girl. I knew it was the right thing. I hoped it was the right thing. But I couldn't watch her leave. I had to stay in the hotel.

Chorus 5 *(Daisy's mum)*
I had to watch them take her off. I kept waving at her while I could see her face and then I just kept waving at the car. Until it disappeared round the corner. Maybe this wasn't happening. Maybe she'd just gone to the shops like she did and would come home tonight. She wouldn't of course. This was it. She was gone. She would come back. One day. But not until she was ready. Until they said she was ready. 'Your child is safe tonight' it says on the web site. Was she? Would it work? Would she ever forgive me for this? Maybe she will be back in time for our holiday in Italy.

Daisy
I could see mum waving at me as we pulled away. She cried but she didn't wipe her eyes. I don't think she wanted me to realise she was crying. But I knew she was. I didn't cry. I wasn't ready to cry. I turned around and just looked straight ahead. She probably stood there and waved the whole time the car went into the distance. I wasn't going to look back. Not now.

(Throughout the previous monologues Dad should sit at one side of the space with his head in his hands, Mum waves and cries facing the audience while Daisy 'drifts' further and further away)

Daisy
When you get to The States; because they don't want your parents to come and get you or they don't want you to run away they blindfold you for the next leg of the journey.

(Chorus 2 and 3 put a blindfold on her)

I've always liked being blindfolded.

Daisy
(Lifting up the blindfold to address the audience directly)

No! I don't mean like that! Behave yourselves!

(She puts the blindfold back on and remains standing still while the whole of the chorus joyfully move over to the chair where 'dad' has been sitting and start singing 'Happy Birthday to you' to an empty chair as if the five year old Daisy is now sitting on it)

Chorus 5
Look at mummy's big girl now. Can you count the candles on the cake with mummy? One, two, three, four, five. Well done! Daisy is five today! What a special girl you are! Can you blow them all out in one big puff? Take a big breath. After three. One! Two! Three! Wow! What a clever girl!

Chorus 2
Let's play in the tree house!

Chorus 5
Would you like Mummy to bring your cake and pop up to the tree house?

Daisy
Yes please Mummy!

Chorus 3
Come on Daisy!

(Chorus 2, 3 and 4 grab Daisy's hands and they skip around the stage. They sit down together)

Chorus 4
Look what I've made for you Daisy! It's a daisy chain! *(She mimes delicately holding a daisy chain)* A daisy chain for Daisy.

Chorus 3
Put it on! Put it on!

(Chorus 2 carefully places the daisy chain around Daisy's neck)

Daisy
Don't break it! Do I look pretty?

Chorus 1
Let's play pin the tail on the donkey! Look! Daddy's drawn you a special donkey.

Chorus 5
It looks like a cat.

Chorus 1
Shut up dear.

Chorus 5
A dead cat.

Chorus 1
Spin her round. Round and round.

(While the chorus mime doing this to the five year old Daisy the 'real' Daisy spins herself around)

Chorus 5
There you are. Now pin the tail.

(The chorus cheer her on as the 'real' Daisy mimes pinning the tail. The chorus laugh)

Daisy
(Using a child's voice)

Let me see! Let me see!

(She rips the blindfold off)

I put it on his bottom! I put it on his bottom! Like he's doing a poop!

Chorus 5
Daisy!

(They all freeze)

Daisy
There'll be no more pinning tails on Donkey's bottoms for me for a while. Although I did get cactus needles stuck in my bottom when I was in the desert at RedCliff. That was bloody painful I can tell you. More bloody painful than having a tattoo, that's for sure. Another girl pulled them out for me. One by one.

(Daisy bends over as Chorus 3 come forward to mime pulling the needles out)

Daisy
Fuck!

Chorus 3
Sorry Daisy.

Daisy
Shit, that hurt!

Chorus 3
Only two more to go.

Daisy
You're joking.

Chorus 3
Nope! Sorry! Here goes!

(The next one comes out)

Daisy
SHIT!

Chorus 3
One more! Here goes!

(The last one comes out)

Daisy *(To the audience again)*
Anyway. I'm jumping ahead

In a State

Section 2

Chorus 5
Turning points
Cross Roads
Cross Words
Steps forward
Steps back
Two steps forward
One step back.
One step forward
Two steps back.

(Cheesy American accent)

You do the math.

Chorus 4 *(As a leader of RedCliff Ascent. American accent)*
Good morning team and welcome to the new student briefing.
We have quite a few recent applicants to consider. So here goes. Student
A is a heroin addict. Simple as. Parents were heroin addicts. Committed
various serious offences to feed the habit. Burglary. Burglary with
assault. Extortion. Breaking and entry. Always a common thread of
violence. Sometimes extreme. Student B. Dad runs a very successful
restaurant. Charming man on the face of it. Entertaining. Sophisticated.
Married to the job. His wife has been left to bring the child up pretty
much alone. Child kicks against the system. Mum can't cope. Dad
doesn't care. He's never there to care. The usual vicious spiral. Student
C. Witness to domestic abuse. Now in care but playing merry hell.
Student D is also in care but was taken away from teenage parents as a
baby. You've all got the notes.

Daisy
And then there was me. Would you send your child off to spend a few
months with this lot? Maybe not. But don't look so disapproving.
These guys at RedCliff knew what they were doing. Although I have to
admit 'Heroin Girl' was pretty terrifying. I was shit scared of her.
I thought I was tough. I punched a total stranger in the face once. But
this girl. Believe me, if you think you've had it tough in life you've never
met 'Heroin Girl'. She shall remain anonymous to protect her identity.

(Whispers conspiratorially to the audience)

And to protect me in case I ever see her again.

Chorus 2 *(As a leader at RedCliff)*
The tools and materials you need to make a fire are all around you.
And listen carefully! If you can't make a fire you don't eat hot food.

Daisy
Ooh! I'm good with fires. Maybe now's the time to own up about the
science lab fire.

Chorus 2
First you need a bow about 18 to 24 inches long. You can cut it green or find a dry branch, but make sure it's strong enough and has a little flex to it. At one end it needs a notch in it.

Daisy *(As young Daisy to Chorus 4)*
Meet me round the back of the Science labs. The window's broken there an' we can get in the prep room.

Chorus 4
Why?

Daisy
Durr! Prep room. Chemicals. Drugs.

Chorus 2
And then you have to attach a piece of string from there to this end like a semi-circle. Make sure the knots don't slip and loosen the bowstring.

Daisy
There must be something there to get high on.

Chorus 2
Then you'll need a spindle and you've got to wrap the string around it like so. The spindle should be about half an inch thick and 4 to 8 inches long.

Chorus 4
No shit!

Chorus 2
You'll need a palm rock to apply down pressure on the fire board.

Daisy
It's freezin' in 'ere. Light that Bunsen burner.

Chorus 4
No way!

Daisy
I will then.

(Young Daisy lights the burner)

Chorus 2
And you put some nesting and coal on your fire board like so, and put your foot on it and start spinning the spindle with the bow whilst pressing really hard with the rock.

Chorus 4 *(Miming picking up a big glass bottle)*
What's in here?

(She smells it)

Wow! That's sick Daisy. Smell that!

Chorus 2
Don't forget to blow it

Daisy *(Fumbling with Chorus 2 and the bottle)*
Shit! You've dropped it!

Chorus 2
And then you get a fire!

Daisy
Shit it's on fire! Get the fuck outta here!

Chorus 2

Remember! Bow drill fires are ninety percent preparation and ten percent perspiration.

Daisy

As opposed to science lab fires which are zero percent preparation and a hundred percent shitting your pants. But they should've thanked me. The science labs were shit. In the winter you had to light Bunsen burners just to keep warm. They got new labs on the insurance thanks to me. Anyway, when you could make a fire, you could eat. And then you did the washing up. Spit. Dirt. Rub it around and off you go. No Finish with Power Ball action here. As my nan used to say. 'You've gotta eat a peck of dust before you die'.

Chorus 2

Welcome team to today's hike. You all know the drill. We do everything together. We all carry the same kit. Nobody is in this alone.

Daisy

So there we all were. We'd been walking for hours and we decided to make camp. At this point you have to hold on to all your stuff. Your bag and everything in it. It's called part of the cool off period. You have to do a cool off before you can put your stuff down and you have to do this all together. Nobody drops their ruck sack until they're allowed. Can you see where this is going?

(A female chorus member stage left lets her ruck sack drop to the floor. The others look on exasperated. 'Daisy' is played by another female chorus member positioned stage right while 'real' Daisy continues with her narration.)

Daisy

I never liked this bitch. Little Californian surfer type. I'd already had her for picking on one of the other girls, Chelsea. Chelsea was very fat. Chelsea and me became good mates. We still keep in touch. She certainly didn't deserve picking on cos of her size. I made that very clear to this surfer shit. Chelsea needed someone to stand up for her. So when she just dumped her kit on the floor. With no respect for the rest of us. The rest of us who were now going to suffer for her actions. Well, at this point I'd had enough as I was prepared to take.

(Chorus Daisy runs towards ruck sack girl but freezes before she reaches her with her right fist ready to strike)

Remaining Chorus
Fight! Fight! Fight! Fight!

(The real Daisy walks through this tableau)

I ran towards her at full speed. My right foot slipped in the dust but I didn't lose my balance.

(Throughout the following Daisy moves and positions Chorus Daisy's right fist accordingly)

I had a mean right hook. I still do. I've used it many times. I always aim for the nose. Her face exploded.

(The real Daisy slowly positions Chorus Daisy's fist on the nose. Chorus Daisy follows through at full speed. Ruck Sack Girl falls to the floor. They freeze again)

Remaining Chorus
Fight! Fight! Fight! Fight!

Daisy
I quickly climbed on top of her. I pinned her to the ground.

(Chorus Daisy and Ruck Sack Girl again act this out as the remaining chorus shout and physicalise their 'fight, fight' mantra)

Remaining Chorus
Fight! Fight! Fight! Fight!

Daisy

I had my hands round her throat. But she was a strong bitch. She managed to push me off. She came back at me.

(Chorus Daisy and Ruck Sack Girl act this out again accompanied by the 'fight, fight' mantra. They freeze in a grapple)

Daisy

This all happened in seconds. The leaders stepped in to pull us apart.

(Two chorus members now move in pull the girls apart. Real Daisy positions Chorus Daisy's hand to grab Ruck Sack Girl's hair)

Daisy

They were working hard to pull her off me but I held on to her hair and pulled her back the other way. The bitch got it from both ends.

(Transition to night time with Chorus 3 (a camp helper) and Daisy lying on their backs looking up at the stars)

Chorus 3

Do you need to go and speak with the counsellor?

Daisy

No.

Chorus 3

I think perhaps you should.

Daisy

I think perhaps he's an arsehole.

(Beat)

Chorus 3
Do you respect yourself for what you did today?

(Daisy shrugs)

Chorus 3
But you've started to find self-respect. I've seen that in you. You're a Leo aren't you?

Daisy
Yeah.

Chorus 3
Hercules killed the Nemean Lion, represented by Leo, during his first labour. You can see the constellation by following the pointer stars of The Big Dipper to the bright blue-white star Regulus in Leo's chest. Can you see it?

Daisy
Yeah

Chorus 3
Hercules was famed for his brawn but his wits needed improvement.

(Long pause as the two of them continue to look up at the stars)

Chorus 3
You do realise you won't be going home just yet?

(Daisy shrugs)

Chorus 3 *(Sitting up. To the audience)*
Daisy just shrugged. I didn't think she'd take this so well. It meant she wouldn't be joining the rest of her family on holiday in Italy.

(She lies back down)

Daisy *(Sitting up. To the audience)*
I just shrugged. I was heartbroken. I so much wanted to go to Italy with my family but I wasn't going to admit to it. When I went to bed that night I cried myself to sleep.

Chorus 1 *(Dad. Putting his arm around Chorus 5 as Mum)*
Darling. Daisy won't be joining us on holiday.

(There follows projections of a family holiday in Italy while Daisy sits with her head in her hands and Dad just keeps his arm around Mum. All set to a music track)

Daisy
Rebecca was just one of the helpers but we made a connection.
I avoided the official counsellor as much as I could. I told him to fuck off more than once. He never minded. He told me that he understood why I was angry. That just pissed me off even more. But I liked Rebecca. She gave me my Earth Name when I eventually left. Earth names sum up who you are and the progress you've made. It also gives you something to go back to when times get tough. Something to think about and focus on.

Chorus 3
Daisy you have been on quite the journey since you arrived here at RedCliff. You came in a closed off, hurting, angry girl, began your journey experiencing lots of highs and lows and have started to develop into a confident, vibrant happy young woman.

Chorus 3

The Garnet is a beautiful stone that when red symbolises passion, energy, confidence, and inspiration. You are full of passion and energy. However, be cautious to not let them carry you in a negative direction. Instead, let them lead you forward as you have learned to lead others with positive thoughts and into social success. On the other end of the spectrum when it is green in colour the Garnet represents serenity, patience, meditation and creativity. Learn how to balance these two aspects of the Garnet.

It may be a small bird but the Starling doesn't let its size keep it from being heard. It is naturally a very sociable bird, but its manner can also be forceful at times. The Starling's ability to communicate diversity and opinion aids it as it navigates the wide open sky with freedom and independence.

The Earth symbolises growth, and Daisy, you have shown a great deal of growth since you first set foot in this wilderness. You have grown more open emotionally, more aware of your actions and their impact on others, more conscious of your words, more confident in yourself and as a leader in your group.

To help remind you of what you have gained we would like to offer you the name Garnet Starling Embraces the Earth.

(The Chorus embark on a sequence of devised repetition of 'Garnet Starling Embraces the Earth')

Daisy's return

Section 3

Daisy

By the time I got back and started my new school, that's senior school number… number 4, it was close to Christmas.

(She lies on her tummy writing in a diary. This could be produced from the ruck sack)

Chorus *(Singing like choristers to The Twelve Days of Christmas)*
On the third day of Christmas Daisy sent to me

21 fucks

68 fags

And 12 and half missed lessons

Daisy

It's my new diary. I keep it under the mattress. Mum and Dad don't know. It's to try and keep myself on track. By fucks I don't mean fucks as in sex. I mean fucks as in swearing to teachers. The fags is obvious. As is the missed lessons. The half was because I went to the toilet half way through Geography and ended up having a fag behind the music school. Make that 69 fags. But it's all better than it used to be. In my old school, before I went to America I never went to any lessons. That's why I got kicked out. Well, that and setting fire to the science lab.

One of the first lessons I went to in my new school was Drama. That was going to be a challenge. I actually liked Drama in my old school but I hate those ponsy games they all insist on playing. They make you feel so stupid.

(Chorus 2 comes out as the Drama Teacher and Daisy joins the line of the remaining chorus in position 5)

Chorus 2
Morning Year 10. We've got a new pupil with us today. This is Daisy everyone.

(Shy and muted welcome by the pupils)

So let's get to know each other a bit. Help Daisy get to know our names. Let's play a bit of a game.

Daisy
I knew it.

Chorus 2
Some of you will have done this before.

Daisy
I bet they have.

Chorus 2
It's where you have to introduce yourself with an alliterative pronoun and a mime. For example I would be Jumping Jones.

(He jumps as he says this)

Carry it on Chris!

(The chorus go on to introduce themselves with suitably cheesy mimes)

Chorus 1
Crazy Chris.

Chorus 3
Jumping Joe.

Chorus 2
I did jumping. Do something else.

Chorus 3
Oh, er, Jazzy Joe.

Chorus 2
Well done!

Chorus 4
Wriggly Will.

Chorus 5
Barmy Beth.

Daisy *(To the audience)*
Now at this point I have several options. I either do it and look a complete twat like the rest of them; or I claim shyness and decline. I know! Me! Shy! Or I simply tell Mr Jones to fuck off.

(Beat)

Make that 22 fucks. I could keep score for cricket matches, me!

(She amends the diary)

He was such a prat though.

Chorus 5 *(As mum)*
Hello darling. Can I come in?

(As she enters Daisy's bedroom, Daisy hides the diary)

Chorus 5
What's that you've got? Homework?

Daisy
It's private.

Chorus 5
That's OK darling. I just wanted to see how school was.

Chorus 1 *(Dad but not in the bedroom. To the audience)*
I told her not to go up.

Chorus 5
How was your first week?

Daisy
Ok.

Chorus 1
I knew she wouldn't get anywhere.

Chorus 5
What are the other pupils like?

Daisy
Ok.

Chorus 1
If you push Daisy too far she'll just clam up.

Chorus 5
What's your tutor like?

Daisy
Ok.

Chorus 1
Or explode. I was waiting for it.

(Beat)

But she wasn't the one who exploded.

(Beat)

(Chorus 5 turns to face Chorus 1)

Chorus 1
I told you not to go up. You've gotta give her some time.

Chorus 5
Time! Time! Like the sort of time you've given her commuting to London every week?

Chorus 1
That's unfair.

Chorus 5
It's not unfair. What's unfair is you telling me when I can or can't speak to my own daughter…

Chorus 1
I haven't said that.

Chorus 5
… after she's been in a fuckin' boot camp for six months.

Daisy
I could hear them downstairs. I hated this. It was just like before I went away.

Chorus 1
It wasn't a boot camp. You know that. And we both agreed to it.

Chorus 5 *(Mimicking him)*
'And we both agreed to it'. Don't be so fucking childish.

Chorus 1
I'm not being childish.

Chorus 5
And stop whingeing.

Daisy
But this was different. I could cope with it. RedCliff had taught me that. Rebecca had taught me that.

Chorus 1
I'm not whingeing. I'm being very calm. And you know it wasn't a boot camp. Daisy had some good times there.

Daisy
I did have some good times. Apart from the pine needles. And the fight with Californian Surfer Bitch.

Chorus 1
She had some good times. She's on the mend. But she still needs her space.

Chorus 5
Yes, Mr fucking psychiatrist. 'On the mend'. What's that supposed to mean?

Daisy

There was a time when this would have made me feel guilty. Like it was my fault they argued just cos I wasn't in the mood to talk to mum. But not now. Lot's of parents argue. It's not the kids' fault.

'The journey in between what you once were and who you are now becoming is where the dance of life takes place.'

It's a Native American proverb. It's beautiful. The dance of life.

(Physical Theatre/Dance routine set to music possibly representing school life for Daisy on her return)

Daisy

I've gotta be honest. My return to normal education wasn't a bed of roses. But it wasn't a disaster. I had now been reduced to petty crimes such as swearing at the bus driver, wearing trousers to school instead of a skirt, the headmistress hated that one and using the staff toilet. I got caught doing that by the French teacher, Mr Bagman. What a name! Big fat old bloke who always had a bad chest and even worse breath!

(She becomes Mr Bagman)

Young lady! Have you been granted permission to use the staff facilities?

(As Daisy)

'Staff facilities'! What sort of shit is that?

No, I haven't.

(As Mr Bagman)

'No, I haven't'! (getting louder) 'No, I haven't!' Young lady I think you meant to say 'No, I'm very sorry Mr Bagman.'

(As Daisy)

Daisy

No, I'm very sorry Mr Bagman

(beat)

But I'm having my period and I just needed to get in somewhere quick.

(To the audience)

That's always a great one with male teachers. He went bright red and coughed and spluttered and squirmed away muttering something about not doing it again. Even in today's modern society male teachers can't deal with that one. They can't disprove it. What are they going to do? Make a note on their wall planners? *(imitating Mr Bagman again)* One month from today. Check if Daisy is having her period. *(Back to being Daisy)* It's just not going to happen. But the year came and went and I stuck with it. Just about. Garnet Starling and all that. And the next year came around. And I sort of started to calm down. Drama lessons took a turn for the better. There was one where we did some work on Shakespeare. I never thought I'd see the day I'd be in a Shakespeare lesson but there you go.

(She gets a piece of paper out of her pocket and reads the next line from it)

Henry the Fourth Part One.

(She screws up the paper and throws it into the audience)

I knew I'd never remember that. Anyway, Shakespeare wrote this scene where this guy, this Prince or something, was in the pub, a place very close to my heart. And he was going to be in trouble with his Dad when he got home. A situation very close to my heart. So, his mate, I can't remember who, a fat old guy, says to him 'You be your Dad an' I'll be you an' I'll show you what to say to him'. And we had to do it in a modern way.

(Daisy reclines in a chair as a chorus girl creeps across behind her on tip toe as if she's Daisy coming home late. Just as she passes…

Daisy *(As her Dad. Mock deep voice)*
And what time do you call this?

Chorus 3
Well dad, there's something I need to explain to you.

Daisy *(Still as dad)*
Explain! Explain!

(To the audience as herself)

You can imagine the way this developed.

(Cut to the end of the lesson)

Chorus 2 *(The Drama Teacher)*
That's the end of the lesson. Great work guys. Well done. That's a great technique to use in your own work. Explain where it comes from and you get even more marks. Remember! Copy from the best and you don't get much better than Shakespeare.

Daisy *(Under her breath)*
Or Chekov.

Chorus 2
Or Chekov

Daisy
He says that every time.

Chorus 2
Excellent work Daisy. Some of the best I've seen from you.

Daisy
Thanks.

Chorus 2

You've got an amazing story to tell. You're pretty inspirational.

(Daisy just shrugs.)

Chorus 2

No, you are. You've been through some amazing experiences. Tough experiences. And you've come out the other side all the better for it. You should be proud.

Daisy

Other people have it a lot tougher than me.

Chorus 2

Maybe. But that doesn't take away from what you've been through. From what you've achieved. You should write it down. It'd make a great play.

Daisy

I'm gonna miss my bus.

The Final Item in the Bag

Section 4

All of the chorus form a line facing the audience wearing the masks which they wore in the opening. These will obviously need to be retrieved from wherever they placed them. Unlike the opening Daisy stands slightly in front of them in the centre. She doesn't wear a mask. She has her ruck sack with her again.

Daisy

Enigmatic Daisy.
The girl behind the mask.
Charming
Open
Brutally honest.
Then masked
Behind beguiling poker face.
Smiling,
Laughing.
Then masked
Dispassionate and cold.

A wild horse in the desert.
Where trust can be earned
But so easily burned.
Burned by a parent who pushes too far.
Burned by a counsellor
Flying too close to the flame.
Burned by a lover
Not wanting the same.

Enigmatic Daisy
The girl behind the mask.
The girl still learning
To leave the mask for burning.

Each chorus member now proceeds to take off their mask. As they do so they say their line and hand their mask to Daisy who places it in her ruck sack. This symbolises the key markers in her journey. Each chorus member then picks up a chair and sits facing Daisy as if they are the front row of the audience.

Chorus 1
I taught her how to smile.

Chorus 2
Excellent work Daisy.

Chorus 3
My little sister.

Chorus 4
I nicked it from Tesco.

Chorus 5
Can you count the candles?

Daisy
Look at this! Everyone sitting here watching me. Daisy. Like I've just been awarded some prize at speech day. I haven't. What do you think this is? Some cheesy Hollywood movie? *(Mock cheesy American accent)* And we would now like to award Daisy with the school's highest honour. *(Back to herself)* Highest honour my arse! This is the girl who still wagged off maths last week to sort out makeup and clothes to meet my mates in town after school. Drama lessons took a turn for the better. Mr Jones stopped playing those stupid games. Although I did refuse to speak to him at the end of term when he didn't make me Drama Prefect. I gave him the cold shoulder for a few days for that. I still know how to make a point. But who cares? I've already been awarded an honour. The best honour. My Earth Name. Garnet Starling Embraces The Earth. What sort of Earth Name would you deserve? Think about it! I mean it! It makes a difference. As for me. Well, sometimes I'm the Garnet, sometimes I'm the Starling. But I'm always Daisy. *(She winks at the audience and leaves)*

The End

RedCliff Ascent

RedCliff Ascent was founded in 1993 and provides a therapeutic wilderness programme for troubled teenagers aged 13-17. It is based in Southern Utah USA and is not a boot camp, adventure camp or any other kind of camp. Their model is based on respect and trust.
They don't just hold therapy sessions outdoors they understand how to use the environment as a clinical tool. Their goal is to help families find solutions to the struggles they face at home with troubled teenagers and to build pathways to success. In The Daisy Chain the scene where Daisy's sister researches RedCliff Ascent incorporates quotes from the RedCliff website www.redcliffascent.com.